Darkness and Snowfall

by
Andrew Fox

Carnoustie
Blind Serpent Press
1989

First published by Blind Serpent Press
18 Ireland Street, Carnoustie DD7 6AT
Scotland

ISBN 0 9511678 3 9

Printed by The Acorn Press, Carnoustie

nh\90

Acknowledgement is made to the editors of the following magazines
and anthologies in which some of these poems first appeared:

*AMF, Blind Serpent, Chapman, Gallimaufry, New Writing Scotland 5,
Samizdat, Seagate II and Voices International (USA)*

Some of these poems also appeared in "The Oceanographers",
published by the Rusty Harrow Press in 1985.

The publisher acknowledges subsidy from the Scottish Arts Council
towards the publication of this volume.

TO

HAMISH AND BRENDA

CONTENTS

ODE TO MY DOOR KEY

You match a lock five hundred miles
from here and will end the silence
of this journey when your serrated tongue
speaks its unique language and connects
me with a living face.
                                    For twelve years
my thumb and forefinger have rubbed
away your alien roughness and your
colouring has mellowed to honeyed
stone.
                    But though the lawns here are neat,
the roses grow strong and tall, you can
open no doors, can speak no privileged
idiom in your cold monogamy.

You are a stranger here yourself, a tourist
in a hungry town, though your relationship
with the world is stricter than mine,
who must travel to discover how I stand
with those behind the door you open.

TROPICAL STORM WITH TIGER BY HENRI ROUSSEAU

In this submerged dominion
orchids are grown
                under pressure
and trailing ferns undulated
by the languid rhythms
of the breeze,
till
crack of lightning snaps like bone
      and scatters the flies on
a drenched honeycomb.

The downpour quickens from blurred
cascade to wild applause
of rain,
flickering in the slippery blackness
      of the forest; the big
pendulous drops slide under
the forked branches
and fall
slowly into rippled pools. A paw
      squelches in the wet,
the tip of a tail curled
around tail
with feline precision, the sinuous
      line of backbone
running to neck.

              Striped fur prickles,
a spark of lightning darts along
his brush and he sees
a tiger
leaping from the darkened canvas, feels
      the pinch of claws on his
chest. Fear boxes his ears
with silence
as he

struggles to the window, slams the shutters
    against whitewashed walls, looks
out on the Paris sky-line
with eye of tiger
terrorized in its lair.

FOR HUGO BARBER, DROWNED

I do not know how your boat capsized,
or how you were flung into the loch,
I have only imagination to guide me.
Of how you had been told several times
to learn to swim, how when you stood up
abruptly during a solitary fishing trip
you lost balance and fell in
with a splash
a sudden hiccup of white
as if some strange bird were alighting.

No one saw from the stony margin
your naked arm vanish
although it was the last time
you would be seen or known as a man.
Down you went, your fisherman's jersey
loaded with bubbles; likewise your boots
and socks; with your fish-hooks and flies,
a curiosity to those fish you might have
caught; gradually losing your name,
becoming part of legend
                          the fool
who can still be heard of a summer's
evening
murmuring for his Peggy.
                          You turned
over in your sleep like a turning wave
and entered one of sleep's many channels,
always the vague traveller; you turned
over in your sleep, reached out
for your wife and found yourself dead:
one of the numberless waves stunned
and broken by the shore.

COMMANDO

Once he was young and eager
before death surprised him
in a solitude which thrives on pain
   and turned his skin to feathers.

Now he lies prone on the rippling sand
in the open grave of the desert,
compassed by the foothills of a broken
       helicopter
which form his horizon: his ruined America.

Burnt to a shade, large quills prickle on
the surface of his back where the flesh has been
torn away until the muscles show. The stuffed
head is preserved
    by a silver helmet naked
of insignia. On his scorched wrist
a digital watch
    stolen by a streetwise kid
who ducked into the army to escape the law;
a lean hoodlum wasted,
      transformed into
his own inept wings: of feathers, wax and string.

RAIN

Rain moves like a shadow
over the suburbs.
              The rain is beautiful,
though not to the gargoyles on the steeple
nor to the shipyard cranes
                     that stand
on one leg;
             it is beautiful to those
who lie in a house like a rock unshaken
and listen to the downpour
                  as it splatters
the flags,
         prickles the moonlit park
and crazes the curtained windows
with a noise
           like brown paper being
crumpled.
            On the roof there is an uproar
as intimate as thunder in a wardrobe
while I lie back
             under the open window
and feel the breeze on lips and tongue,
smell the cool tang of rain.

DENTIST

Waiting for the injection to numb
and pouch my cheeks the dentist
picks at my teeth with a long
probe looking for more fillings.

"Open wide. Wider," he says and
manipulates his angling equipment
in my mouth, hooks the nozzle
of an air-jet over my lower lip

as if I were a giant fish hauled
up from the depths to the surface
glare of a spotlight, the blue
elbow with its steel pinion above

me. The masked nurse sits with
a faint rustle of nylon, the cool
uniform resists her golden flesh
when she leans over to adjust

an air-jet, her eyes like green
almonds. My arm touches the channel
of her thigh as I quietly dissolve
on this plastic couch and wait

for the insistent needling of the drill.

BABYLON

Babylon the great
has fallen,
            a white flash razed
its bright domes, changed
the walled city
into
a hold of rapid demons, a cage
of silent lips,
a plague of golden locusts.

We are men no longer,
but flame
            and the ghost
of flame. The heat
shudders
inside a chrysalis
            until the membrane
breaks into a black flower
grown fat
upon human slaughter.

We mourn for the light,
for the birdless
vacancy,
for the crippled merchantmen
buried in the harbour.

AT NIGHT

At night death comes tapping
with his leather head, his limbs
like twisted sticks of hickory.

He is the toppled wicket strong
enough to check the brightest sun
as it rolls along the runnel

of a ledge, like an orange with
an eye soaked in blood, and drops
with a sickening knock knock

at the door of my skull.

HELEN

Meanwhile smoke rose from a single chimney,
a mongrel loped against the palace wall,
and a boy tilled a field
whistling. Once
or twice
he stopped his curved plough, wiped his palms
       and looked up
at the white cumulus clouds. Terns
balanced easily on the river,
half lost in shoals
of light. Old
men snored
in the meadow. Among the reeds
a swan discovered
something
and reared in splendour, pumping the black
     shadow of its wings. No
doubt the boy never heard
the human moan hidden
in the swan's
brief
shout or saw the bruised girl slink away
     ashamed, a robe draped
between her plucked breasts. There
was no one to prove that day
a swan and girl
had made
a swan's daughter, a solemn child,
who scampered after chickens
in the yard, explored
the sharp reeds
and ate
peaches beside the scintillating river until
the moon pulled at her blood
and princes sailed
in tarred
ships from distant archipelagoes

                    to court a legendary mistress
in a bare chamber. She watched
her suitors leave, hare-lip
and hunchback, never
losing
her composure like an empty jar

poised on a sill.

MISS STUART

The garden was overgrown,
barely contained
inside
the boundary wall; interlocking branches
     choked the sunlight. Beyond
a terraced lawn the workman laid
the grass with a scythe
and a pigeon
walked
among coils of perished hose. I entered
     the derelict house by an open
door, the dark hall smelt
of mould, climbed
the staircase
down which
Miss Stuart tumbled fifty years ago, her
     skull fractured by a man
she picked up in Monte Carlo:
then looked into rooms
furnished with
light.
     From a window I saw the birds in
the orchard below, the blue river,
and the Cricket Ground on
Cavendish Road.

TO A FLOWERING CHERRY

At Pentecost I burnt my old letters
while a flowering cherry broke into speech,
the moving lips of the blossom
in one accord
with the suave blades of light.

A feast of alien tongues crinkled in
the eager flames and turned into wet petals
of charred paper;
                        petals that will always
cling to me until I throw in

my lot with the blaze
and let these strange flowerings prevail
over empires that herald winter.

MEMORIES OF EDEN

When I enter the Victorian Swimming Baths,
by the swing doors, my pebbled
lenses steam up. I half
expect a tropical
garden:
instead iron branches proliferate under
      the glass ceiling, tendrils
bear rusty flowers which droop
in the heat, and opulent
foliage
curls further with each white belly flop,
      each plain or swallow dive
into the turquoise pond.

A pale boy is grabbed by his fellows
and thrown without ceremony
into the deep end. He
pedals briefly
upon
the air, then breaks the crystal water
      with a splash. The pool
fluctuates, a green
meniscus
dips by the overflow, black lines buckle
      inward, coincide and cross,
filaments of light
chase
after the limpid waves, lick the edges
      and rebound upon the fallen
swimmer, his sleek hair
combed, his cool
eyes
roundly pressed. He is the exile
with a double crown
whose
flesh trembles underwater like the thin
      hemisphere of a bubble. I watch

the reflections upon the glazed
surface and the square
tiles wobble.
                    The water is whole,
but what I perceive is distorted:

I cannot tell which shapes are real.

THE OCEANOGRAPHERS

Financed by a baby powder millionaire,
the white submersible is launched
from the stern
of a recovery vessel. The pilot and I sit
                inside an acrylic
sphere, gently aware of its
soporific weight,
                ailerons trimmed,
sonar tuned constantly
to the active
mode.
          The only noises are the turning ribs
of the scanner, the ticking of my gold
watch, and the pluck pluck
pluck of bubbles
              on the cabin while
the swollen vehicle bumbles
deeper into the gloom,
                clears the barricade
of a wreck and plummets into a canyon
like an electronic shard fallen
from the 20th century.

Over four hundred fathoms below
I have regained
            the pleasure of pure being,
am once more like dolphin or
porpoise. Cameras map
uncharted regions
              less familiar than
the moon. We follow the ocean bed,
trawl for octopods
             or pursue tile
fish into their burrows. Steel
pincers bristle among
transparent
shoals,

fringed hermaphrodites and polyps
with five foot streamers.

Warped in the lens of a glass bowl, I
carry even here
                my frail assumptions,
the burden of holocaust and war. My
cockpit sinks over tangled forests,
luminous with the fires
                of unknown
creatures. I am the stranger,
the mysterious predator
who descends,
captured in a globe of light.

PRUDENCE AND THE STARS

During the night
a meteor
plunged behind the derelict barn and made
          a deep hole in the brown
meadow. Prudence rose up
and followed
                    the pieces of star which
jumped away over the shaven field
like crickets.

One particle
grilled a brook to its pebbles; another
                         became lodged in
the fork of an apple tree: she
picked its speaking fire
from
the branches and nursed the burning fragment

in her lap

like a frozen bird. Sparse hedges bristled.

PARABLE

This stubborn tree in flower
eludes the deepest
        gaze,
deceives as it consoles the eye
    and seems to follow
precepts of its
        own

when after a period of splendour
        the petals are trampled
down and the resinous
scents dissolved
in the rain,

leaving branches concise
in their elegant
hold
of the blue air

using the least means to prevail.

CIRCUS BELLE

She hastens like the bright tail
of a comet
               across the tented darkness
from trapeze to trapeze
a tenuous flame
lured into the unreality of flight
                      eaten alive
by the iridescent spotlights
and the diamond eyes
of the audience
as they hold their breaths
                  caught up in reveries
of her poised belly curve
anxious lest she fall
yet wanting her
to fall on to the sawdust below
                her mind vacant
as the solitudes she nightly
inhabits.
               She is one of the neutral
of the earth who examines
the small biographies
of the crowd
             and does not pass
judgement, more real
than those who applaud her
mind drawn to a point of abstraction
a wave gathered to a peak
                    sharply
defined which bursts in crystal
fragments
            when she slithers
down a rope as though
peeled of a skin

returned to the mundane crush
the muddled sea
                   of shopping bags
and the broken wings of umbrellas.

The canvas lifts and sags. Outside
a makeshift carpark fills with rain.

THE LOST PHOTOGRAPHS

Five months after you left I had the film
        developed,
            but my pictures could not rise through a chemical
                          dusk:
                                now you run like a child
in the night and I can barely remember those final
        hours beyond the pier
     except for the measured utterance of the waves, as though
                        a human effacement
                  had occurred to match the warfare
inside the camera; an adverse reaction by which

the molecules combined to ruin the generous image we had
        of ourselves; even while I followed you back
to the monotonous heat of a parked car.

REMBRANDT, SELF-PORTRAIT, 1632

I shall rise when the candle
        is quenched,
    fill the white pitcher, listen to rain approach
                        on the wind,
                    then regard in the looking glass
a cavalier whose pale head floats
    like a moon
    picked out at dusk.

My contemplation will go beyond
        the upward
    sweep of the wide hat, lace collar, earlobe tipped
                        with light
                    and explore the hidden
structures of grief leaving my person
        intact,
                            mind
                transfigured by the inner spheres:

the harmonies that join the living to the dead.

ASSASSINATION

When he drove the Vauxhall Cavalier
up the ramp
                    of the underground carpark
the bomb exploded. There was a precise,
yet hostile, click as the car bumped
that provocative slope. Onlookers
rushed to the burst vehicle
while the killer
strolled
into the late traffic, the native
    of a country whose interiors
are still unmapped. Within
minutes the victim
had been
zipped inside a body-bag, his widow
                informed, his file pulled
and a collection taken. Within
days his photograph became
less distinct
                in back numbers on
a hundred library shelves;
the firm chin
merged
into its component dots, into the grey
        background of history. He is
not even a footnote, but a carefully
tabulated statistic to be found in
                the appendix of a scholarly
work on the Troubles. He makes
a crooked salute
like
a captain going down with his vessel
    before the sargasso of newsprint
claims him and he sinks back
into a tide of paper.

SLAUGHTERHOUSE

Steam rises from a drum
beside the loading
bay. Spilled

intestines ferment in their own juices.

           I slit the bulge of its
pendulous belly with a thin blade,
open the fat-rolled purse
swimming in blood,
put my fingers
inside
the silken lining and pull down the entrails
feeling my hand warmed up to the wrist.

Attendants loiter on the hosed concrete,
smoking cigarettes expertly
like torturers.
              Pantechnicons are stacked
with nude carcasses, dead caves of rib,
skewered and tied behind
the double doors.

Somewhere, a circular saw whizzes through
bone,
with a cry that might almost be human.

BABEL

After Babel
the human tongue was divided
into many lesser tongues.

But the old speech
remained
like sunlight among the branches,
            even while the new
means of conversation
drove us insane.

Once or twice the dove alighted
and our lips were chastened
by a universal
language
in which neither duplicity nor
            violence
could obtain.

Plovers danced unaware
that we could
understand their metaphors.

The world quivered on the point
of revelation,
                  your face became
clear,
I could see each and every thought,

and my voice slipped into yours.

BLACKBIRD

Often I wake at dawn
and hear
          a threadbare music begin among
the sunlit movements of the pruned
     trees,
each whistle and triple fluting
                    charged
     with an archaic precision, the last note
held a moment and taken up
     in every quarter
of the suburbs, a secret chronicle
     engraved
in bone and the bone's whiteness,

a tune so delicate
the wind might break it
or one false move.

BUDDLEIA

Two years ago the buddleia
   toppled
in the October gales; no one seemed to notice
     the quick frame shaken of birds
        until
     the foliage grew back
around the sloping trunk
  and thwarted root.
         Now
my neighbour talks of its beauty not knowing
what he means
      while I who toppled one night
        like
     the buddleia
look away from the gradual choking, listen

instead
    to the accuracy of birdsong
and the loaded hum of bees.

POPPIES

During the Great War
a private yearned for death until one evening
              he noticed
              the field of poppies which grew
in no man's land, became infatuated
   with the huge
petals light as crinkled silk. Only the black
              pods of opium
              at the centre gave the flowers
their evil weight. For a moment
       he wanted
to reap all that illusory brilliance even the wave
                     upon wave
              of dark stems behind each ripple
of crimson, ached for the colour he
could never own

and did not hear the shot which killed him.

SNAILS

Each night a fresh crop of snails would limp
from the cool beds of lettuce and disport themselves
upon the garden wall, their flesh
neither liquid nor solid more like some abhorrent ooze
or semi-congealed mucus which rippled onward
under the humped shell. By morning
the snails had gone. A rare specimen could be found
beneath the fence where a tap dripped.

Once discovered,
there was a private thrill of horror which edged into
nausea then panic. I would shudder
at the eye-stalks and feel in need of safe confines
beyond which no snail could advance. But
they never stopped coming. Their slime was everywhere.

That was in the year of the snail. Snails
were very prevalent that year.

This evening
when the rain fell among the conifers I touched
a thin web of silver on the wall
and imagined myself a snail
waiting for the birds or the silent boy
with his jam jars.

THE SHADES

in memoriam Martha Sievwright

When the shade plucked
its lyre
the small bones turned in my ears and dark memories
awoke in the subconscious mud.

I had to leave the house at once,
run through an unpainted back door into the garden
and climb the bank. The cold was exact. Below me
in the cutting
railway lines twittered with the approach
of unknown conversations;
and I knew that if I would redeem myself
from whatever ailed
then I must travel down into the kingdom
ruled by Persephone
where the dead confer in their multiple tongues
like starlings. The dead are confused. They
do not have blood enough
to express their knowledge clearly and the living
can never recognize what they are
listening to. Yet we ignore the music of the shades
at our peril.

These pale ghosts look upward
from their catacombs; and in every silence
remember what is to come
for those who achieve that rare alchemy of the spirit:

the light perhaps,

the blaze of light and the noise of leaves.

SOME PHOTOGRAPHS, CIRCA 1910

        In these old Edwardian photographs
the dappled crowd strolls languidly past the Japanese
Tea House, appreciating the shadows
along the fragrant avenues
between the lime trees and the verandahs hung with flowers.

On the Esplanade: billboards advertise Zebra Boot Polish,
schoolgirls watch the light skiffs driven out
beyond the pier,
a striped windbreaker flaps.

The summer heat is cool, the noise of silks
and blowflies muted. A whole perspective dissolves
into the grey still light
of an ocean which, transformed by art,
can no longer hurt its sailors; for the camera
has redeemed the most ordinary lives
because of the shape they made one afternoon
although certain values have been lost
or subtly altered in translation: the blackbird
which chatters alarm from the roof
of the golden belvedere and the tulips poised after rain,
a rain that will level all those elegant heads
now glittering now dark
under the Christ Church Steeple and in the Strawberry Gardens.

BATHSHEBA (AFTER REMBRANDT)

You rise at dawn
    when
his parchment comes, light the candle and read the king's
                request,
             poised on the woven gold of the counterpane,
unable at first to make out the delicate
    Hebrew script
with its elusive turn of phrase.

                 The king tells how
          your body moves under
    the folds of a blue dress,
ocean blue like the mild
voluptuous
breakers; compares the feeling that calls him to
          the particular mystery
of a woman and the ache which
    draws a salmon
back to its native river: the salmon blind in its
        delight. "I do
      not care if death will follow. You
are the destination I carry inside."

"But sir," you will remark
to the officer who climbs the stair, "what about
my child? I listen to him cough at night,
worry in case his breathing
is interrupted."

The guards shoulder their pikes
in the yard below. Wax collects in a brazen saucer. Calm
odalisques walk barefoot in the frost. The king
beguiles you with the private voice of his desire:

"Bathsheba, Bathsheba, come to me naked
      under your blue dress."

THE PLUM TREE

Last year,
when the rain spoiled the plums on the bough,
I dreamt that serpents hatched from the moist plush fruit.

At this point I woke
and felt serpents in the orchard around my crooked house. I
          listened for the black weave and slide
of their flesh. My room was quite still:
the yellow flowers did not
shed their pollen
on the table: and beyond the half-drawn curtain
          I saw the plum tree
which, although it was devoid
of serpents,
stood like an emblem of my own and my country's malaise
          with all its ripeness wasted,
all its fullness gone soft.

I lay on the bed,
observed the plums lose their coherence then drop
one by one into the wet grass
and there was nothing I could do except
watch them fall.

DISCOVERY

Three days after
Miss Adams leapt from the road bridge
a man looking for worms on a beach
down river
turned up a shoe
with her foot still laced inside.

The rain snapped and broke
against the windows. The sun was a black hole
eclipsed by its own light.

That evening
a doctor switched on the Anglepoise
and with a scalpel or some other implement cut open
the shoe. He did not think of the girl
who jumped, her brief memory in water light water,
but how fragile the macabre textures of skin
above the instep; this man
whose knowledge had made him unaware
of the river that winds between the somnolent blue peaks,
the hills which founder in the darkness.

A LOCAL HAUNTING

Each midwinter evening
toward dusk
a ghost walked beneath the derelict asylum among the blue shadows
　　　　　of the wood. The ghost wore a pearl grey
suit. His shaven face was yellow. The white
hair stood crisply upon his head.

Once he stopped in a glade
and listened to the acres of timber creaking, touched here
　　　　　　　the strangeness of a leaf
or a tree exact in all its particulars. Above
the domed observatory the cold ailed him
to his bones, he shivered,
and thought: Heat
is promiscuous, felt almost invisible like a dream moving
　　　　　　as he crossed the gravel yard
and with the quiet irregular footfalls
of the blizzard
entered the asylum where each evening he awoke in a room
　　　　　full of cobwebs: the door was open:
and he strolled from the shadows of memory
into the blue shadows of the wood.

THE ENIGMA

One afternoon
I glimpsed a light between the trees
and followed the light to its source: a translucent space ship
which had travelled from beyond the Crab Nebula
and under whose glass carapace
blue aliens nine feet tall flickered out their dream lives
according to a strange nocturnal logic
that made the cattle uneasy in their pens,
the dogs lose their charisma.

Later that evening I telephoned
my wife Rachel at the Heidelburg Grill, the relays clicked
in exchange after exchange
as she listened to my tale and then without comment
put down the receiver,
wiped her palm on a starched cuff, or meandered back
no doubt through broken crockery
to that squalid kitchen,
never thinking about the silence she left me with:
a silence in which
the shadows closed around me like tar
and pricked by her disbelief I resolved
to bring up my encounter again
when Rachel got home, tell her for example
how the aliens had removed my fingerprints and bundled me
over a crystal threshold
where I stood naked in my little sack of bones.

During this moment of strangeness
she would remain quiet, beggared of words,
because she knows me so well,
because suddenly she would not know me at all,
but watch my lips moving.

A TRUE HISTORY

when my father came back
from the derelict asylum hidden in the forest
he was unable to relate what had occurred
after he was taken
above the broad sweep of the river
to a mansion
that retained a sparse odour of charity and disinfectant
where rats with long skinned tails
scrabbled under the boards
and the other patients were no more than a shuffle of slippers
                            on the waxed linoleum.

one evening
he approached my house through the ancient tangle of the wood.
his boots warped on the snow, but left no tracks.
he returned that night like a fellow conspirator, leaned over my bed
and first tempted then enticed me into the strangeness of evil.
my father could understand neither my spoken tongue
nor the rich amplitudes of my flesh.
i held my paramour in fascination
as he tried to penetrate the riddle of my exquisite suchness
with each bull thrust,
his breath loud in my ear like moist thunder
until he spoke through me
and i could feel the shadows of those enormous depths
in which he was conceived,
depths that change history into myth, the truth into fiction.
i touched bliss,

                            the absolute,
nothing,
my lids half-closed by the five magic herbs of experience.

petals of jade chinked in the wind.

then he vanished,
drifted beyond the single eye of the imagination
and when i awoke, pinched and fretful with cold, it was summer.
wood pigeons lulled the copse to sleep.

that morning i swam naked in the gulf
and my doctor was tantalized
by the most polished of black high heels
which drilled with a rock steady tick tock upon the wooden floor.

tell me doctor,
are wolves still more spiritual than men?

somewhere in the darkness
my father woke, stood on his hind legs and bellowed.

DARKNESS AND SNOWFALL

Last night I heard
an irregular ticking at my window.
I switched off the lamp, pulled open the curtains,
and observed beyond the aquamarine glass
the blizzard alighting everywhere
at once
without alarm to, or the hurried conjecture of,
the animals that hunt in the vacant gardens; no two flakes alike
those intricate elusive feathers tumbled end over end,
were buoyed up a moment, eddied and swirled,
then wavered down past clean spires
past the blue gable of the house opposite and settled
with a faint hiss among the dock leaves
on the moribund ground between the harled walls
and the scribbled tiles.

Once or twice a hesitant flake
approached the warm pane, touched it intimately,
aloofly,
as death had touched the sinners
buried under the Eastern Necropolis;
these few ghost flowers trembled
to be allowed in
and heal the long dark agony of the spirit.

Just after seven o'clock,
when the wind dropped and the silence became impossible,
I went out into the sparse courtyard and lay on a fold of snow;
blinked up at the deft hypnotic petals
which smudged and thawed one by one against my naked lips,
my face scarlet swollen with cold,
until I let myself
be transformed into Apollò's bird, the white swan that hungers
on the dark estuary,
and rose above the uncluttered boughs

above the corrugated roof of the Jig and Tool Manufacturer
upon wings that can shatter a thigh-bone.

I had, in brief, escaped; no one would ever find me again
or the poem ticking inside my head.

THE SPITFIRE

Because sometimes
you must bury your disquiet
in such metaphors
lonelier than a ghost
you enter the oakwood, walk north east
through arboreal shadows,
a shadow yourself,
until you discover the Spitfire wrecked between the trees;
remove the canopy and switch off the radio,
stop it from talking
about armed recces or fighter sweeps; observe
that inside his leather jerkin
the pilot has suffered a mild collapse, his pulped head tipped back,
his flesh transformed into the colours of growing plants
has learned to blend and collaborate
with sweet woodruff, orange phlebia, and white umbilical roots.

Once you believed
that in time even his aeroplane would flower
and its carnal blooms touch
some hidden absolute of experience. But when you turn for home,
pass a lake frozen into stillness, you look up
and see the Spitfire circle these level suburbs, tilt its wings,
then rise above the carriageway and a moorland etched in dry point;
water beads tremble on the cockpit window;
the radio inside talking about
Douai, Nijmegen, or Beauvais Tille; the buckled altimeter
poised at zero.

Behind you
the snow fills the woods with silence
and the moon ripens into blood.